"Love," Written On the Cover...

"Love," Written On the Cover…

- {(Book of Poetry)} -

Kelsey Jan Gaither

|/\/\/\/\/\/\/\/\/\/\/\/\/\/\/\|

• Nashville, T.N.//2022 •

- BOOKS -

|/\/\/\/\/\/\/\/\/\/\/\/\/\/\/\|

To My Friends & Loved Ones,

Whom I Hold So Dear...

— Kelsey Jan

CONTENTS:

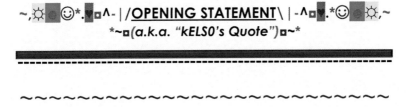

~,☼●☺*.♥□^-||/OPENING STATEMENT\||-^□♥.*☺●☼,~
~□(a.k.a. "kELSO's Quote")□~

~~~~~~

~~~~~~~~~~~~~~~~~~~~~~~~~~~~~~~~

"I want to *make* a **statement** that **stops** *you* in your *tracks*
& makes you *think*…

I want to be *needed.*
      I want to help **someone** make a *difficult* decision.
         I want to **blow** someone *away*…

I want to be *deep.*
      I want to make a **difference** in someone's *life.*
         I want to **take** your *breath away*." **<333**

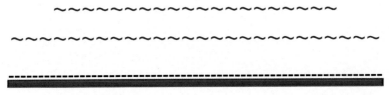

- - - {Excerpt from: *"kELSO's [Black] Book of Poems,"* 2006}.

Poetry Session.

~~~~~~

Memories bleed through by brain
The beating of my heart drives me insane
Pencil to paper and thoughts on mind
I wish I could touch you one last time
Why must my emotions bring me down?
I always wonder when I'll come around
I can't concentrate, I can't sit still
I don't know what to do, so what is the deal?
I am nothing, I am worthless, just another steppingstone
You used me up, then left me here all alone
Get over yourself, you're no different than me
We are one in the same, can't you see?
I am human, I cry and I bleed

Peace at mind, that's all I need.
~~~~~~

Process of the mind - - -
She is cautious with a broken heart inside
Taking life day by day
Facing her fears in hurtful ways
She is broke down and bruised
Trying to heal her own wounds
Making the best of what she's got
Pacing away at life's time clock
Live life and be happy they tell her
She is so sick of those cold Decembers
Trying to forget the memories that haunt
Attempting a smile, but she cannot
Cover it up with a fakeness so golden
She knows it's not gonna hurt when she's frozen
Hollow inside, just trying to make it by
Taking it day by day, trying to enjoy the ride...

---------------------- ***"Happiness is Overwhelming."***

Happiness is overwhelming.
This sweetness takes a hold of me.

Heart is full; head is high.
Never thought it possible till you arrived.

I can't stop smiling when you're around.
There's beauty in the making, so I've found.

Love is the deepest emotion.
And you've given me the strongest potion.

Your inspiration swims through my veins.
That smiling face takes away my pain.

When I hold your hand I feel complete.
If only you could see how you have me at your feet.

Happiness is overwhelming.
This sweetness takes a hold of me. <3

-Remember 987-
("Love," Written On the Cover)

~~~~~~

Something happened that was magical *that* day...
Love flowed over in a *mysterious* way.
Held tight *throughout* the night.
Wake up in the morning,
To a Sun *so* bright.

A *new* journey began,
One unlike *any* other.
The strongest chapter in the book,
"Love," written on the cover...

New day; *new* start...
Heart *so* full; off the chart.
Kiss me; hold *me* tight...
Nothing has ever felt *so* right.

To *let* go would be impossible.
No matter *how many* obstacles.
Love knows *no bounds* in between us...
We can make it through anything,
We must.

~~~~~~

"Things I Love About You..."

Your smile makes me smile;
>   Your laugh makes me laugh.
And when you hold me close & tight,
>   It reminds me that I did something right.
It is beautiful; you & me...
>   Practically amazing for us to be.
Gratefulness cannot describe,
>   The feelings I get deep down inside.
You saved my soul & set me free;
>   I hum around like a happy little bee...

I am at peace;
>   And this will not cease.
On the bottom of the line...
>   You make me happy,
>   And that ends this rhyme.

* ~ . * . ~ - - - - ~ . * . ~ * **<u>ABYSS</u>** * ~ . * . ~ - - - - ~ . * . ~ *

When all you can do
   is stare into the abyss
      of the night...

You scream inside your head,
"Why does nothing turn out right?!"

Your soul is dark; everything feels like a waste.
You look back now
   & don't understand the haste.

Sick to your stomach; head full of pain.

You realize to yourself,
   that nothing will be the same.

Done with hopes;
   tired of dreams...

Your life has unraveled,
   you're breaking at the seams.

"People"

You ever notice how quickly you go through friends in life? Like they are only there for the time you need them... And when you don't need them anymore you just kick them to the curb and move on with your life? Or more so, you just get to know them better and realize how fucked up of a person they truly are. And then there are those times where you just sort of grow apart from each other as time progresses, for no real reason in most cases... It's just how it happens. Every person who has ever been actively involved in your life has influenced you in some way, whether you like it or not. I just find it so funny how people can really help build our character and make us into who we are today. I hate when people won't admit that their friends influence or "rub off" on them. They try so hard to make it out like, "I am my own person." When really you are just a strange twist of everyone you have ever come in contact with, combined with a few miscellaneous occurrences in your life, thus creating your so-called "personality" we now see before us today. True it might be different in some small ways from others, but deep down you're just like everyone else... *So, get over yourself!*

CHAINS

Break *free* from the **chains** that <u>bind</u> you.
I'm <u>hopping</u> *off* this **conveyor belt**...

Millions of *you* being **produced** at a <u>time</u>.
Round & *round,*
    Rolling on the <u>ridges</u> of a **dime**.

I'm <u>done</u> with you **heating** my *core.*
You <u>cannot</u> **control** me *anymore.*

Back *up;*
    You <u>can't</u> touch my **soul**.

You are *meaningless,*
    With the <u>depth</u> of a **black hole**.

"True Romance"

I *am* a romantic. Finally, I've found the answer for my constant desire for *love*. It's a part of my life. My life here on earth is *nothing* without love. I *need* it. I *breathe* it. *Cherish* it. I want to be remembered. *Cared for*. There is nothing *quite* like the feeling of being held by the person you love, to *feel safe*. Feel like *nothing* else matters. Get lost in each other's eyes and *know* you are wanted and needed *right* where you are. Nothing can compare to *that* feeling.

"My Life Story."

I am *not* a selfish person. Every action I make, I have someone *else* in mind. I love and care *more* than any normal human being should. Every bad thing that happens to the people I care about, hurts me *too*. I have *no* talents, *no* goals, or motivations in life. I am *sick* of always being a disappointment. I can't make anyone *consistently* happy... Not *even* myself. All I *am* is a burden. All I have *ever* wished for in life, on *every* birthday, shooting star, wishing well, *every* superstitious scenario, has been for *happiness*. But, it will *never* come...

"A Life without Love"

What is a life *without* love? Dead, *empty?*
What is the point to a life *without* love?
Where would it take you then?
What would you do with your time?
How would you fill that void?
How would you *endure* the pain of *living* a life,
with *nobody* by your side?
Why would you wake up in the morning?
Who would you share precious moments *with?*
Who would you *confide* in?
Who would be there for you to pick your *feet up* off the ground?
What would *lift you up*? *What??*

Nothing. Life is pointless *without* love.
Nothing would motivate you, *nothing.*
This world would not exist *without* love.

Therefore, *Love* is *my* God.
And I will worship it until the day that I die.

*****Something worth worshiping*...

~~*~*~*~*~*~*~*~*~*~*~*~*

Restless Nights

Restless nights,

    Grant me this plea…

The Sun's coming up,

It won't let me be

Headaches & sorrow,

    Fill up the void

And bring me back down

To this helpless deploy…

~~*~*~*~*~*~*~*~*~*~*~*~*

"A Story to Be Told"<3 -

Produce for me an adventure
A new path for the taking
An escape from the coy normality of life
Grant to me a brand of a new beginning
A way to start again
A fresh breath of untouched air
Let it fill my lungs
Sharpness, piercing to the nerves
Show me that things can change
A realistic generic product
Haunting at the thought of the possibility
Force me to gasp,
Make me into a fantasy
Envy the world I crave

Believe in a **story to be told** <3

Kelsey Jan Gaither

"Notice:"

What to do when you don't know what to do with your life? I have *so* many ideas but no clue what to pick, what to follow, or where to start... Life *is* confusing. I never know what to expect next. It truly is unpredictable. I kind of like it that way. It makes it a bit of an *adventure... A lifelong adventure.* I want to be successful. I want to do *great* things, meet *great* people, and have *great* times. I don't want to be held back by doubt, or bad experiences. I want to *flourish* and *grow.* I want to *be* happy... Above all things, I just want to be happy. *Learn. Love. Inspire.* I want to be important to the lives I care *most* about. Be dependable. I don't know if I will accomplish all of my goals, but I know I am going to try my *very* hardest. And as long as I do that, I am at peace with myself. I am proud of what I have accomplished, *thus far,* even though the list is small. I don't know where I'm going with *my* life... But, I do know that it will all work out. Everything *will* be alright. No more worrying...

– Just thought *you* should know.

Kelsey Jan Gaither

"What If's"

"What if's" are the thoughts we have when we feel we've missed out on a possibility... It could have worked out. But, for now you'll never know. It *bugs* you, crawls *underneath* your skin. You wish you knew, but all you can do is weigh the positives and negatives of the road you are on now. You need to either *let go* or *act*. Otherwise, you'll *never* grow...

"Love," Written On the Cover...
Kelsey Jan Gaither
"<u>Journey</u>."

Life *is* hard...
Things are *not* as easy as people like to make it out to be.
It's a difficult realization, but it's one that needs to be made.
It comes as a full package.
The element of surprise is *not* far behind.
You *never* can know what is to *come next...*
You *never* can know where your heart will *lead* you to.
But, it's *always* a *journey...*

An *adventure* that will *never* end.

"L-O-V-E" ~

love [luhv] – *noun*

1. a profoundly tender, passionate affection for another person.
2. a feeling of warm personal attachment or deep affection.
3. a person towards whom love is felt; beloved person; sweetheart.
4. affectionate concern for the well-being of others.

I would not change *one* thing about you.
The *looks* you aim. The *kisses* you give.
The simplex *emotions* you fill my hollow body with.
The *warmth* I feel when you are near.
Even the *stubborn* attitude that shows me an *adventure*...
The way you *remind* me how to *live*.
The reasons to why I still *exist*.
The *chances* we take; the *passion* we make...
I would not change one thing about you. <3

"A Love worth Fighting For…"

What is a love *worth* fighting for? Things get hard in *everything* we do… Obstacles make their way into the picture. How do we know when it's time to *give up,* or when to *move on?* It's so difficult for me to just neglect a feeling *so* real. How could someone just turn their back and hide from something *so* deep in meaning? Something that could grow into a *beautiful* adventure. Why can't people be brave enough to try for *something more?* Something *more* than the usual? I want someone that can see the *worth* in me. Stay *with* me; fight *with* me. *Even* through the hard times, because they see the *big* picture and they want *me* in it. I need someone to love me when I *least* deserve it, because that is when I need it the *most.* A life without love is *not* a life at all. Regardless of life pursuits, I believe *love* should always be a *main* priority. Because, a love *worth* fighting for will outlast *any* commodities. *Maybe,* I'm *just* crazy… *Or perhaps,* I'm a *fighter.*

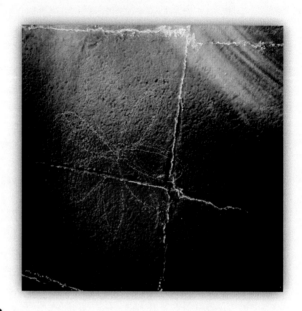

"Dollface"

I'm the doll locked away in your closet.
You have new toys at hand.
You laugh and play, while I sleep away.
Dreaming of days *long* forgotten.

The seasons change, you've lost my name.
My heart is as dead as cotton.
My hands are cold, clothing ripped and old.
Dreaming of days *long* forgotten.

I cannot cry, I have no feelings to find.
You tossed away the key.
Left me here in my insanity.
Dreaming of days *long* forgotten.

One day, I may come across your mind.
The others, they will help you push me aside.
I'll sit here and wait, fearing a long debate.
Dreaming of days *long* forgotten.

Simplify<3

("Path of Which We're Bound")

~~~~~~

Simplifying the heavy lives we live

Happy with the effects we give

Measuring out each other's reaction

Until we've met our satisfaction

Unsure of how to convey

The words we've yet to relay

Tiptoeing around,

The path of which we're bound... <3

~~~~~~

"Two Sides."

I have had *my* fair share of depression. I've been through a lot of *shitty* things, dealt with a lot of *shitty* people, seen and experienced a lot of *horrible* things. I've cried, my heart has *ached...* My body has *shut down* on me. I've *abused* myself. I've *abused* the people around me. I *have* regrets... I *have* hatred.

But, I have *experienced* happiness... I've been through a lot of *amazing* things. Met a lot of *amazing* people. My heart has *swelled* with joy. My body has *shivered* with hope. I have *laughed* like there is *no* tomorrow. These are the memories that will *never* escape me.

For a while, I don't think I *even* knew how to act happy. I didn't know how to show my happiness even if it was there. I was so use to the illness depression brought *upon* my soul that I didn't know there *could* be anything else... I *am* learning. I *am* growing. I don't have to be sad. I don't have to be lonely. I *have* loved. I have *been* loved. I *have* love, and love is the *best* thing this world has to offer. <3

Happiness~ {("Backwards & Forwards")}

Perhaps, I could live in a world,
a world of *abnormal* happiness.
Where things happen *backwards* & life *fast forwards*...
You discover why all the little things *finally* add up.
The people you've developed bonds with *all* give you input
on the life you are destined to have.

You can travel the globe & find the same *irony*
from *coast* to *coast.*
The same lessons being learned.
The same people all under the *same* body & skin,
with the same heart being chipped *away* at from *day* to *day*...
The *same* insecurities *being* unleashed.

Figuring's being done to decide what it is we all *truly* want in life.
Meeting the needs that, perhaps, we *don't* need met at all.

You tell me what *you've* learned,
& tell me of the people *you've* come across...
Have they not all had *one* thing in common?
All of our wants & needs are to meet the *same* prophesy.
We all just want our *own* piece of sanity.
Our *own* form of happy. =) <3

"Life"

Life is *weird*. It has a *funny* way of working itself out. It takes you *around* in circles. It *hurts* you, *leads* you on... And forces you to discover happiness in the hardest, *most* complicated way possible.

Slipping... ("Things You Forgot")

You forgot to do the things you wanted

Didn't say what you needed to

Let too much time pass than you should have

Left things unsaid that should have been spoken

Left people behind that need to be here now

Life is slipping........ *slipping*

"Love," Written On the Cover...

Kelsey Jan Gaither

"Midnight..."

I think the world of you,
And I'd like you to know
The many things, I cannot show.
It's always been you
That should be mine,
But we were good
And we took our time.
One never knows how things like this begin...
I'm just happy we don't have to pretend.
In a world where people like you exist,
Is the very thing, I will always insist.
I'm so thankful you are who you are
And I can validate, that I will never stray far...
No one could ever want any more than this.
Always loving you,
         Until the candle desists. <3

"Love," Written On the Cover...

Kelsey Jan Gaither

Some Mommies ("A Mother's Day Poem")

- -

Some mommies make kids breakfast
Some mommies tie kids' shoes
My mommy gives me hell,
That's <u>RIGHT</u>!!!
& makes me cry, *"Boo Hoo..."*

She bitches & moans when things
At home do not go exactly her way
She'll hold you down
& make you frown
Until you clean up the *decay!*

My mommy is not around too much
Other families look like such a happy bunch
My mommy says, "Just give them a *punch!*"
...That will be the day

My mommy has tough layers
She could probably run for mayor

She'll pick a fight & tell you to,
"Get outta her sight!"
My mommy's <u>such</u> a riot...

Some mommies care too little
Some mommies care too much

My mommy cares just enough
To make my heart go, *"Crunch!"*

Some mommies run their kids away
Some mommies want motherhood to end...

Well,
That just really *sucks* for them!
...'Cause my mommy's my <u>Best friend</u> <3

- -

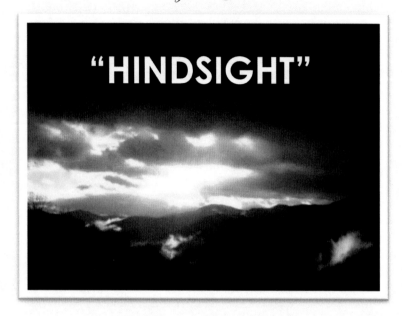

When *he's* <u>gone</u> *she* sees in **black** and **white**.
    The **moon** is <u>dull</u>; the **Sun's** *not* as <u>bright</u>.
<u>Across</u> the **world** *he* floats around;
    He can't find a **place** to put *his* feet on the <u>ground</u>.

She holds *her* head <u>high</u>, as *she* tries <u>not</u> to cry.
    Impatience– *she's* never been well with <u>time</u>.
He feels <u>jaded</u>, under-compensated.
    Emotionless– is the *best* place to <u>hide</u>.

Both are <u>blind</u>;
    Ridden with an <u>overactive</u> mind.
Everyone *knows* what's **plain to see**,
    That <u>these two</u> are *meant* to be.

No other *two* **lovers'** hearts <u>are</u> as such.
    No other *two* **love** each other <u>quite</u> as much.
The <u>worst</u> *tragedy* in the **world**;
    Was the day *he* decided *she* <u>wasn't</u> *his* **girl**.

xoxo.crossmyheart<3

X's & *O's* across my chest.
I *just* can't seem to give it a rest.

It is for you *I* live & *I* breathe…
I promise to *always* wear my heart *on* my sleeve.

Taking chances... & falling apart.
Never giving up, *my* love is *an art.*

True men, there are only *so* few…
Everything I do, *know* that I do it all for *you.*

When I find you, I shall *catch* you with a *net!*
My *true* love, I have not *yet* met.

"Temporary State"

Life is *only* a temporary state of being.
We are *never* promised tomorrow,
So we *must* live to the *fullest* today.
Do what you *love;*
Love what you *do.*
And *always* remember that,
"Every passing minute
Is *another chance*
To turn it *all around..."* <3
~ *(Vanilla Sky, 2001)* ~

"Change" <3

Always be open to *change.*

Every day, I grow *wiser.*

Every day, I grow *stronger.*

I am *always* allowing myself room for improvement.

I am aiming to be the *best* possible version of myself

that I *can* be, while *still* remaining true to myself.

I am grateful for the things that I *have.*

But, at the *same time,*

I am grateful for the things I *don't have.*

Cane ("Follow Me")

Take me back to that <u>bliss</u>.
He is standing there loving *me*.

I can feel the <u>wholeness</u> of my heartbeat.
My eyes are *fading...*
My mind is *bent*.

Build me *up* to break me *down*.
Swallow me <u>up</u>; hollow me <u>out</u>.

I am <u>used</u>... I am <u>broken</u>.
Rub salt in *my* wounds.

I will still *press on...*
You are a <u>blind</u> man, and I am your <u>cane</u>.

Follow me...

~*<u>Favorite Things</u>*~

~~~~~~~~~~~~~~~~~~~~~~~~~~~~~~~~~~~~

Smoke clouds on lipstick && dizzy remissions,

Bright city lights && boyfriends I'm missin'...

Friendships forgotten && Red Bull wings!

These are a few of my favorite things!

Paintings that call you && laughter that grips,

Sleepless nights && endless road trips...

Blissful moments && words that may sting!

These are a few of my favorite things!

Making mistakes && growing old,

Never forgiving && then growing cold...

Relentless rebellion && finding you're insane!

These are a few of my favorite things!

When my glass drops, when the music stops,

When I'm feeling sad...

I simply remember my favorite things,

And then I don't feeel *so bad!!!*

~~~~~~~~~~~~~~~~~~~~~~~~~~~~~~~~~~~~

"Girl like Me!" - - - - - - - - - - - - - -

And don'tcha wish you had a *girl like me?*

Keeping you satisfied,

Blazed with the *maddest* life.

Let go.

Embrace the *depth* of my endless attraction.

You know I love it when you *give me that reaction!*

Engage in my *wonder.*

Without *me,* life is a blunder.

A *mess.* There is no contest.

Take it or leaveee.....

Get *lost in my mind!*

Give me a moment, to show you *that you're mine.*

Fulfilling *everything,*

You could ever need...

Baby, you know you wanna *girl like me!*

- -

"Our World."<3

Take me somewhere that I can run.
I want to feel the breeze and the Sun.
I want to know peace inside my heart,
Contentment to keep me away from the dark.

Take me away from the bitterness and hate.
I want to enjoy the bliss, until we meet our fate.
I want to live my life with the freedom of love,
To do things for the fun... jus' because.
I want to know at the end of the day,
Someone will be there to hold me and say...

"No matter what, everything will be okay."

Where Are You Now?

You say that you loved me, but *where are you now?*

You used to be there for me,
But I've lost you *somehow...*

Your words were like diamonds, glittering with hope.
Now, I see all my efforts must have felt like a joke.

I gave you my whole heart,
– Nothing <u>less</u>. Nothing <u>more</u>.

Was returning the favor so much of a chore?

After everything that's happened,
    I don't know why I still believed...

That for once you might say, something you really mean.

You say that you loved me,
    But *where are you now?*

Never again will you obtain me.
– This is my <u>solemn</u> vow.

It was childish of me, to put so much trust in you...
    Though, I thought I had found someone who may be true.

Now, I find myself alone,
    Exhausted and *meek.*

You say that you loved me,
    Next time think before you *speak.*

"Dreamt of You"~

I dreamt of you last night,
& for a moment it almost felt real…

I woke to a world I could not
      find myself in
            & shook at the appeal.

The busy sounds & explicitness
      drove me away…

& all that was left
      was a memory,
            long washed away.~

"That Which Doesn't Kill You, Only Makes You Stronger..."

No matter how old I get, there are still things in this world that I will never be able to understand... & these things tend to frustrate the *ever-living shit* out of me.

I've *always* tried to speak my mind & be as honest, as possible. I've seen & experienced *more* hardships than any human-being *ever* should. I've seen single parents *struggling* to raise their kids & put food on the table... Children *fall* to abandonment. The rich get *richer* & the poor get *poorer*. People physically & mentally abused *without* rhyme or reason. Good people *fall* to addictions. Death come in families *long* before it should & the effects caused on the people *who loved* them the most...

So many unjustifiable tragedies, & *so much* heartache, trauma, & pain. From these experiences stems a passion, so great in me that I hardly know how to control it. I just want to impact & change the world *so* badly... *(**1 mind at a time**)*. For the sake of the *greater* good. But, bashing & name calling is *not* the way to seek results. I'd rather *lead by example,* be a *source of inspiration* & a *force to be reckoned with,* than a bitter hateful prune. **My greatest asset is my most flawed weakness...**

And even though, *at times,* I may not always make it clear, know that I have *all* the love in the world for you -- **Even those I don't** *fully* **understand or** *agree* **with.**

I will always be constantly *learning, changing, & growing...* *Even* at my *lowest of lows,* know that this girl will *never* quit.

Each day, I *only* grow stronger... A *true* fighter. I'll keep going 'til the heels of my feet *turn* raw.

Endless Horizon.

There's so much I've wanted to tell you,
   yet couldn't speak the words...

But, darling know this,
   you've always been the *Sun*.
      The <u>Source</u>.
         My <u>Muse</u>.
That which *illuminates*, & *adds*
   definition to the *meaning of my life*.

You are the <u>center of my being</u>;
   The *gravitation of my thoughts*.

A <u>beautiful view</u> transpiring
   across an *Endless Horizon.*<3

--That which I <u>set my sights to,</u>
   as I move *forward*
      <u>towards</u> the *future...*

"<u>Beauty</u>."~

What is beauty to you?
Is it appeasing to view?
Does it achieve physical perfection?
Start a war...
Send ships across the sea?

...Or is it something you can *hold*?
Touch, Feel in your heart,
& *Know*....

When the day is done & years have passed,
Will it remain the same?
Does it defy all odds,
& overcome all obstacles?
Put aside all selfish
& materialistic desires?
Bring *happiness, peace, tranquility*?
Is it more like *love*?

Love... in all the meaning of the word,
– Now that is beautiful.

"The Past."

You know, I've been scared of the past & what I might find there... I've gotten so use to having these walls up, that I haven't been sure how to take them back down. I went through some old possessions trying to clean things out to make room for something new. And what I found was *no* matter how hard you try to run from it, the past is never far behind. It's an interesting thing when life manages to come back around full circle & you find yourself right back where you left off. You can't let what has happened in your past make you afraid of *what's to come...* It's time for me to get back on the road again. It's time to move →→→ *FORWARD*.

"Lights" -

Lights on the edge
Of a horizon

Moonlight showing
the way

Waves crash
Stars twinkle

Clouds scatter
across the sky…

"Love," Written On the Cover...
Kelsey Jan Gaither

Out of the darkest of nights, I'll lead you from the frustration...
The moon rains over us, acting as a beacon from the devastation.

A beam could almost pass its way through,
    if the earth were set in motion.

I've been at the **bottom**,
    had to climb my way *back up*...
Held more **determination**, *than a warrior* <u>seeking the cup</u>.

<u>**Felt & Seen**</u>,
    with *hardly anything* in-between.

Blisters formed at the *rawness of emotion*...
Like <u>little pockets of disintegration</u> **echoing at the notion**.

It's a funny thing to find,
    when you think you've <u>put in</u> *the time*...

Yet all *my **capabilities***,
*my **strengths**,*
even *my **weaknesses**,* helping to guide this <u>**Iridescent Soul**</u> of mine...

Add up to nothing, if I can't learn to ***let go***.

And so, if you feel your **heart inside you**, *draw me near.*
I am facing my fears.
I hold you close, <u>every single day</u>.

I care for you more than my words or actions could <u>**EVER**</u> convey.

And even though you are not everything I had wanted...
I still feel a **pull** to you *gravity couldn't* <u>even stomach</u>.

You *remind me* of the **simple things**,
I tried <u>**SO HARD**</u> not to forget...

Thinking of you brings a comfort to me,
    like a <u>morning bird</u> *singing a sonnet.* <3

<u>*Regardless*</u> of all I've been through,
    nothing could have prepared *me* for *you*...

No matter how much I try to deny,
    you are the ***Rise*** to my ***Fall***, the very <u>rarest</u> of them all...

I love you *more than* could **ever** be known,
    and *nothing will compare* when this <u>knowledge</u> takes its **toll**.

"Growth"~

Forever growing;

Forever learning.

I'm sorry for the wrong I've done.

I'm sorry for the people I've hurt along the way...

I'm sorry for not being there for you when I should have.

I'm sorry for shutting doors when I shouldn't have.

I will *never* be a perfect person.

But, I will *always* keep trying.

I *hope* we all have great lives...

I *hope* we all reach our dreams.

I can *never* stand to see a person I care for down and out.

I *really* do wish the best for *each* and *every* one of my friends.

No matter what you're going through,

Know that things will *always* get better.

Be *grateful* for what you *have*...

~~~~~~

Life is *beautiful*,

Never forget that.

~~~~~~

Stay positive.

We're *all* in this *together*.

You are *never* alone. <3

"Conscience."

My conscience will be the *death of me;*
It *haunts* me while I sleep…
I know the things I want and need,
But these tasks I just *cannot* complete

I'm *not* who I *used* to be
I can see I'm *not* the same
But, when I take a look around
…I'm the *only* one to blame

The clock is riddled with faces & names
Of people *no longer* around
I'm *not* even sure, why the pictures *so* lure;
My memories can't *even* be found

Was I *ever* happy?
Was I *always* this way?
Maybe this is my *true* self…
A fragile-hearted little loner,
Who can't stop kicking herself

I've wasted *so* much time,
Believing in my rhymes…
The days keep *slipping away*

Where did I go wrong?
Where's that melody to my *Ravenous Everlasting Song?*
My heart aches *each* and *every* day

The world's broken me down,
And I can't *seem* to turn it around
It gets harder *each* step of the way…

I block it all out and work towards my goal,
But *even* then, I still have nothing to show

I'm *smart enough,* I'm *brilliant,*
I'm *sane!*
But *regardless,* still nobody remembers my name

Alone in a world that didn't want me from the start
Left with myself, *falling apart…*

~•◊\\ - - - - - - - - - - - ▫ *"**Jigsaw//Pieces**"* ▫ - - - - - - - - - - - //◊•~

Take me back to *my* roots…
My system *just* can't *seem* to compute
A strangle that *cannot* break free
I'm longing for the moment of its release

I've been holding on for what feels like *so* long…
They say the night is *always* darkest before *its* dawn
Contemplated a device to help matter desist
It's feeling, *as though,* I will *never* get past this…

Echoes & *bellowing,* like the wind through the trees
I wish *those* Novembers would *just* let me be…
Take me *away,* free me from this disdain
A place called, *"home,"* keeps calling *my* name

Who am I kidding? I've been through it *all*…
In need of a revision, to this great *rise* & then *fall*
Winter will *only* be here *too* soon
You know the cause of this *deep* monsoon

Reason has *only* gotten me *so* far,
Nothing could set things higher than this bar…
Everything in life has added up to this…
Jigsaw pieces to meet a consist

Smile in frame; I'll *always* remain the same
Promises, *promises,* never forget my name
Love is the *most* complex emotion
Pushing & *pulling,* like the waves of the ocean

"Love," Written On the Cover...
Kelsey Jan Gaither

I'll *X & O* all over your chest…
Swear that we will *never* give it a rest
You get *my* back, & I'll get *yours*
Swear that we can make it to shore

Like I've said, *time & again*…

This is *only* the *beginning,*
Please give it an *end*…

Pariah*~

Will life *ever* be complete? Always working towards a goal; even when you have it all, it feels like something is missing... No matter *how* hard I try, there is still always work to be done. It's *never-ending.* I pray for contentment, but it's still *never* enough. I don't know what the point is anymore. I've lost my way. I look towards the future & it's only me I see, standing there *all* alone... What's the point to this all? *Every* day I wake up, I get lost in the anxiety & fear of my *entire* world crumbling to the ground. I know why I started this, but *why* am I to finish this now? When it's just you, there is no point. There is nothing here to share. I mindlessly go through the motions of everyday life, working towards my *never-ending* goal... Just when I think I've made a dent in it, 10 more things pile up & fill the empty space. I feel like I'm running *in* place. I keep *slipping & falling...* I *can't* move forward. I'm *so* scared of failure, I keep burying myself in my work. Just *one* more page, just *one* more project... The next thing you know *years* have gone by...

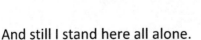

And still I stand here all alone.

I feel like I've wasted *so* much time. I hate working *so* hard, investing *so* much of myself into something & finding it to have *no* point. I'm terrified this *whole* thing has been a waste. This town has *aged* me. The harsh reality of life has hit me *full* force. I hate *what* I've become. I need things to get better... I just want my *old* self back. I'm scared I'll never be the same. My thoughts center around my anxieties, & it all engulfs me *so*... I can't *rise* above. I keep *sinking*... Drowning into my books, & the *never-ending* projects. I've been hoping it will all pay off, that it will all be worth it in the end.

"Well, this is *what* it takes... If you want the life you want to live, then this is what you *must* do..."

The stress is just all *too* real. I'd feel like a complete failure *without* this. What *else* am I to do? I keep working towards my goal...

I'm not happy anymore. I'm barely *even* here... I fade in & out, I'm scared I *won't* come to. I just keep working through the days hoping everything will sort itself out. I *try* not to think; I *try* not to feel. "Just get your work done," I tell myself, "don't worry about *anything* else..."

And *so,* more time goes by,
And still I stand here all alone.

"Love," Written On the Cover...

Kelsey Jan Gaither

"Love," Written On the Cover...

Kelsey Jan Gaither

"Untitled" ---

I've been through hell & back
I've got nothing to prove...
I still carry on, no matter how bruised
There is so much more to all of this
I see it every day, I feel it so deep
I walk around & take a look,
And the beauty makes me weep

Trying to put myself back together it feels...
I've been in pieces far too long
I lost a part of me I know it
Broken off, stranded, can't find where I went wrong
Running in circles, constantly in second guess
Head humming with a questioning
I thought I'd always know best
I keep moving, I keep my head up
Sometimes, it just takes time
Impatience gets the better of me,
I forget to enjoy the ride

Little signs get sent to me,
I can hear it in a song...
It touches my heart, opens me up, and for a moment I feel I belong
Exactly what I needed, it brings some confidence to myself...
Things are never as bad as you make it out to be
Your perceptions got you twisted, feeling caught up in a dream
When you finally get to see all your struggles paying off
There's a reassurance to this mess of a game,
Racing against life's ticking time-clock...

I don't know where I'm going, but I know where I have been
And nothing could compare to the place I was back then
Someone's got my back; I can feel it in my bones
I know that wasn't me that did this all alone...
Deep breath, then I'll start it all over again
Even if I fail, I'll find a new place to begin
I see the positives; my work hasn't all been a waste
Sometimes, the ground feels like it's spinning,
I'm still a bit wobbly on my feet
But, I can't wait to slow it down,
And then maybe find some peace
Life is really not that complicated when you stop and do the math
I'm tiptoeing on these steppingstones, but I know I'm on the right path...

"Everything for a Reason..."

Everything happens for a reason.
Everything we've ever been through in life,
Every person we've ever met,
Every experience we've had is for a *purpose*.
It makes us who we are today.
Without it, we would *never* be the same...

You take *all* of the good, with *all* of the bad.
If you didn't have the *negatives* in life, you wouldn't see the *positives*.
Both are needed.

No matter what you go through in life, *no* matter where you've been,
As long as you're a good person, keep good morals,
& *stay true* to yourself...

Everything *will* be okay.

But, you can *never* give up. Don't *ever* stop trying.
When you stop trying, that is where you *falter*.
That's when things *turn* sour. That is *when* you *fail*.

Don't *ever* give up on yourself... *Always* try for more.

Everyone in life is given their *own* individual test.
We each have our *own* purpose & importance in life.
Not everyone's test is the same.

<u>The One.</u>

If I could make a list
You'd meet every *one*…

My thoughts turn to *you*
Like the rising of the Sun

Winter *becomes* Spring,
Then, Summer to Fall

Just going through the motions
Trying to take *on* it all…

Some *come & go,*
Yet, here I *still* remain…

Searching for *the one*
Who can take away *this* pain…

I know that *one* day,
Things will eventually go *my* way

Waiting for *the one*
Who will love me *the same*…

"Cheshiring..."

Fading *in & out,*
Hard to ascertain what it *is* that is *real*...

I'm *somewhat* here,
Then, *somewhere* gone...
Can't find where *I'm* supposed to belong!

Standing on the in-between;
In *two* places at *one* time...

Head *humming* with a frequency,
Pulling me *back & forth,* then *side to side*...

My eyes are seeing double;
& I'm finding *all this* to be of *much* trouble...

Not sure of what it could *really* mean...

I'm *cheshiring,*
& it's the *most strangest* thing!

What *is* real life,
As we thought we *once* knew?

Perception's surpassed what was *thought* to be *true,*
& no longer are things how they *once* had all *seemed*...

Maybe, *perhaps,* this could all have been *some* dream?

"Stuck." ~ ~ ~ ~ ~ ~ ~ ~ ~ ~ ~ ~ ~

Stuck in <u>one</u> place,
<u>Ready</u> to move *along*...

Been following a <u>dream</u>,
I've <u>chased</u> for *so* long.

Feet feeling <u>weary</u>,
My *own* <u>personal</u> hell...
Start <u>second guessing</u>, *fearing*,
"What if, <u>somewhere</u>, I went wrong?"

<u>Waiting</u> for the pay off,
Not sure <u>how</u> I get through *each* day...
Been <u>looking back</u>, *wondering*,
"What if things <u>won't</u> be the same?"

When <u>will</u> this *end?*
When <u>will</u> it *stop?*

The *<u>beating</u> pound,*
Of this *ticking* <u>time-clock</u>...

Could You Be?~ *{("Soulmate"<3)}*

I think about you at night...
When I lay down in my room
I think about what *could* be
Our destiny's *only* presumed

Could you be the *one?*
You feel like *home* to me...
I'm lost in a paradox
This feeling of drifting out to sea...
Do you remember how things were?
Do you ever think it *could* be?
Perhaps, you were the *one,*
The *one* meant to be with *me...*

Get lost in each other's eyes once more
...I'm *simply* drowning away
Sometimes, I miss you
& I can't pinpoint why...
I wish you'd stop with the delay...
I'm *in* love with the idea of you
Where's my, *"Happily ever after?"*

Everything ends in *disarray*
Maybe, we're trying to avoid *disaster...?*
Have you found someone new?
Is it anything like *could* be,
Us, *me & you...*

I just want someone good by my side
There's no end to the range,
Of an *onslaught* of people,
That could *never* fill your place...
It's so significant, *me & you*
Please, tell me *what* it is?
This draw I feel between us,
Like the Sun *submits* to the moon
Am I *too* hot-headed?
Do I bore you *pretty* babe?

"Love," Written On the Cover...

Kelsey Jan Gaither

We play catch-up *once* more,
Why can't it be the same?
What if you were the *one?*
What if we were it?
We could spend our *whole* lives
Dancing around it...

It doesn't matter what we do
We could restart from the top
Who knows *what* lovers do?
Our love *could* be *nonstop...*
What are you hiding from?
What is with the wait?
I feel it will all *too* soon, be *too* late
You *could* hold off a *million* years
My love would feel the same...
Maybe, we're *not* done yet
Reason *still* remains...
Maybe, that's *not* the ending,
Heart beckoning for *answers*
Why are we pretending?

Do you remember how things were?
Do you ever think it *could* be?
Perhaps, you were the *one,*
The *one* meant to be with *me...*

What If? ("Drowning") --

What *if* it was you...?
Here comes *that* thunder
Turn your back on me now?
Leave me standing there,
All alone, rain pouring down...
The *worst* has *just* begun
You think *I'm* strong?
Do you *think?*
Tear my heart to pieces...
Get it over & done with
What's the point to it *all* now?
Tell me *this*...

Who were *you* to judge?
Who *am* I?
You don't see
You don't see *me*...

Some friend are you?
What about family?
The river runs *shallow* with *this* one...
A rocky slander
Head caving down
Tell me *when* it's over...
Deep breath, *start* again
How many *more* times?
Glad you found the energy for this
Push *me* under
Push *me* down
I'll be drowning now...
Searching for air
You could *never* compare
What was this? *Pointless* fun?
I've been *over* this <u>since '91</u>...

"Love," Written On the Cover...
Kelsey Jan Gaither

<u>TIME</u>

. . . .

Take a look at your life,

Is it everything you hoped it <u>would be</u>?

I stood on a mountaintop,

And I screamed, *"<u>Let it be</u>...."*

The work, the busyness;

The people just couldn't see...

Their lives were engulfed,

By everything that *could* be...

You see others smile & laugh...

You want things to change,

But you can't change your past.

The stress, the worry,

"Will everything be okay?"

It's all still the same,

By the end of the day...

"Love," Written On the Cover...

Kelsey Jan Gaither

You'd throw your whole life away

Working at some dead-end job...

Then stop, & look back,

But now, you can't turn the knob...

The door is shut,

And someone tossed away the key...

Well, tell me this little one,

Was it everything you hoped it <u>would be</u>?

Live in the moment,

Appreciate the time...

Eventually the clock will run out,

And you'll be left with this façade...

Be good to one-another,

Love as much as you can...

So many people waste their lives,

And just cannot understand...

"Why can't I <u>be happy</u>?"

"What is this <u>life worth</u>?!"

You forgot the most important part,

<u>You</u> coming *first*...

Don't <u>waste</u> your time,

Don't forget what I've said...

<u>Love</u> is the answer;

And <u>happiness</u> goes with it,

Joining, <u>hand-in-hand</u>. <3

"Finally"~

◊ - ◊ - ◊ - ◊ - ◊ - ◊ - ◊ - ◊ - ◊ - ◊ - ◊ - ◊ - ◊ - ◊ - ◊

Finally, I am *free;*

I can just *let* things be...

These headaches and sorrow

Won't get the *best* of me.

Freedom from *heartache;*

Freedom from *pain...*

It's times *like* these,

You *know* you're *not* the same...

Finally, some rest;

Finally, some peace...

It's all you could need,

In hard times, *like* these.

Smiling faces;

Over joyed...

Let this be *forever,*

And *finally,* set *coast* to the *shore.*

◊ - ◊ - ◊ - ◊ - ◊ - ◊ - ◊ - ◊ - ◊ - ◊ - ◊ - ◊ - ◊ - ◊ - ◊

"This Is The Last One..."

Time stops for *no one*. Life is *forever* one big surprise. Expectancies sometimes can *never* be met. No matter *how* hard we try. No matter *how* much we give. No matter *how* much we are *even* capable of achieving... Regardless of our beliefs on what *should* be *given* in return. God has *His own* plans. Life has its *many* twists and turns. I search for stability. Consistency. An understanding & reason, *somewhere,* in this world. In the *chaos* that can surround us.... *Even* our roots can't save us now.

Our pasts can *still* come back to haunt us. No matter *how* far you think you have come. No matter *how* much you believe, maybe, *perhaps,* you have escaped. Made it out alive. Overcome. The bitch of the thing is shit can *still* pursue. More can *still* occur. Just when you think that *finally* you are done... He hits you with *one* big, great *last* one... A *final* test in time. I don't know *what* You *have* planned for me. I don't know *who* You believe I *must* be to take on something *like* this. Superwoman *couldn't* do this. Wonder Woman would *be* perturbed... *And as for* me, I shall search for shelter & guidance to get me the rest of the way *through* this.

You've *never* forsaken me before. I *do not* believe You will forsake me *now*. Goodness will *always* be met with reward. And I *am* beside myself. With *nothing* left in me to give... With *everything* I've *been* through & done, up until *now*. I know *this* is the *last* one.

I *pray* for strength...

Be good. *Always* look out for one-another. *Never* believe that you *are* alone. I love *everyone*. I believe *in* everyone. *Never* let the bad ensue. *Rise* & be *anew*...

"Love," Written On the Cover...
Kelsey Jan Gaither

The End.

Poem Bio/About the Author:

Author/Poet's name is Kelsey Jan Gaither—*(also known by her pen name, Kelsey Jan)*—and was born on July 12, 1991. She was raised in Tennessee and currently still lives there today with her cat Zahari... "I came from a low-income, single parent home In my teenage years, I started writing poetry as a coping mechanism to help me better deal with my severe clinical depression, as suggested by doctor. In my youth, I was the quiet and reserved type, and poetry helped me get outside of myself a little more, by writing my innermost thoughts and feelings down onto paper—allowing me a positive source of outlet and means o self-expression.

I began using my poetry writings as a way of journal keeping, writing about major life events by using vague and symbolic metaphors and rhymes to express my deepest, innermost thoughts and feelings on pressing matters—something like writing in code. Later in life, once I had battled and eventually overcame my severe issues with depression, my poetry then shifted from the dark distraught, and more heavy-felt, deeper topics towards more of the lighter sense of topics— *involving personal over-comings, peace, and overall, love.* As my relationships and bonds grew deeper and stronger, they also took that of a more serious tone, as comes with time and age.

My writing is always left somewhat abstract, as to allow personal interpretation for each of its readers. I love the art of how one person can read one thing and apply it to their own personal life and get something out of it, and someone else can read the same exact thing and get something completely different out of it, than that which the other person did. Every poem I write is like a little piece of myself, parts of my soul, and often depicts a serious topic, event, or challenge within my own personal life.

In college, I began as a major in 'Philosophy,' wanting to study the great minds of famous thinkers of our past and expand, or explore, upon specific personal interests and ideas within my own life. I later, however, changed majors—my good eye, great sense of taste, and love for aesthetics won out and I chose 'Interior Design,' as my main career field. My great interest and deep-seeded love for creative-writing never has ceased, though. I still continue on with my personal writings in my spare time, jotting down little interests and ideas, making rhythms and rhymes as I go...

I hope my writing has the ability to incite and cure the thoughts and minds of its readers. Containing highly-relatable experiences and issues within its descriptions, so eloquent and simplistically written as to leave no confusion to its readers, making it possible for any person to relate and understand the topics explored in this poetry collection piece."

Thank You for Reading!
~Kelsey Jan ☺

****
KelseyJan.Designs@Gmail.com
KelseyJan.LiveJournal.com

◊ More Books by the Author ◊

~ Kelsey Jan Gaither ~

~~~~~~~~~~~~~~~~~~~~~~~~~~~~~~~~~~

– Poetry Book Collections –

Kelsey Jan Poetry Series:
(Book 1 & 2)

"Love," Written On the Cover... {(Book of Poetry)}
kELSO's [Black] Book of Poems: A Poetry Prequel

– Children's Novels –

A Fairy's Tale

– Additional Publications –

Poem, "TIME," seen in book, *Walk of Life: Anthology of Poems*,
by Poets' Choice, in year 2021, p. 67-68.

~~~~~~~~~~~~~~~~~~~~~~~~~~~~~~~~~~

Made in the USA
Columbia, SC
17 February 2023

12164365R00044